Exploring Physical Science
Exploring
FORCES AND
MOTION

Andrew Solway

rosen publishing's
rosen central

New York

Published in 2008 by The Rosen Publishing Group, Inc.
29 East 21st Street, New York, NY 10010

First Edition

Editor: Vicky Brooker

Cover photograph: Christian Lagereek/istockphoto.com

Photo credits: p. 5: istockphoto.com; p. 9: Shaun Lowe/istockphoto.com; p. 11: Mario Tama/
Getty Images; p. 13: Andreas Steinbach/istockphoto.com; p. 15: TRL Ltd/Science Photo Library;
p. 16: Stock Montage/Getty Images; p. 17: Lester Lefkowitz/Getty Images; p. 18: Eric Bechtold/
istockphoto.com; p. 19: NASA; p. 21: Porsche; p. 22: Three Lions/Getty Images; p. 23: NASA;
p. 24: NASA; p. 26: Jeff McDonald/istockphoto.com; p. 27: NASA/JSC; p. 28: Library of Congress;
p. 29: NASA; p. 31: Chris Fairclough/cfwimages.com; p. 33: NASA; p. 34: Clive Rose/Getty
Images; p. 37: Anthony Taylor/istockphoto.com; p. 38: William Farquhar/ istockphoto.com;
p. 40: Pierrette Guertin/istockphoto.com; p. 41: Chris Fairclough/cfwimages. com; p. 43:
Edward Parker/EASI-Images/cfwimages.com; p. 45: Pascal Goetgheluck/ Science Photo Library

Library of Congress Cataloging-in-Publication Data

Solway, Andrew.
  Forces and motion / Andrew Solway. -- 1st ed.
     p. cm. -- (Exploring Physical Science)
  Includes index.
  ISBN-13: 978-1-4042-3747-6 (library binding)
  ISBN-10: 1-4042-3747-X (library binding)
  1. Force and energy--Juvenile literature. 2. Motion--Juvenile literature. I. Title.
  QC73.4.S66 2007
  531'.6--dc22

                              2006036680

Manufactured in China

Contents

CHAPTER I

What is a force?

Simply put, **force** means something that pushes or pulls. In fact, every push, pull, twist, stretch, and squash is caused by a force. Forces hold together the tiny **atoms** that everything is made of. Forces keep Earth in **orbit** around the Sun, and forces are behind all kinds of motion. If something starts moving or stops, it is because of a force. If it goes faster or slower, or changes direction, there is a force at work. Whatever is happening, on Earth or in space, it is certain that somewhere there is a force making it happen.

Forces and motion

In this book, we will look at the many different ways that forces can act. Sometimes it is obvious how a force acts. If you push a toy car, it moves forward. If you pull on a drawer, it opens. In other cases, the forces are not so obvious. What force keeps socks from falling down? And what forces act on a parachutist floating through the air?

Forces and motion are closely linked. In this book, we will look at how to describe motion, and how to measure it. We will also look at **friction**, the force that opposes movement.

 FUNDAMENTAL FORCES

Physicists have shown that all the different forces in the universe belong to one of four basic kinds. These are **gravity, electromagnetism,** and two atomic forces called the strong force and the weak force. Gravity is what holds us on Earth, and keeps Earth in orbit around the Sun. Electromagnetic forces include magnetic force and the forces behind all chemical reactions. The strong and weak forces hold the **nucleus** of an atom together. Without these forces, the parts of an atom would fly apart.

Harnessing forces

Today, we can harness many forces to work for us—electricity, magnetism, chemical forces, even the forces within the nucleus of an atom. Our way of living depends on machines that use these forces. We also use many simple machines to make work easier. Everything from tweezers to tower cranes rely on simple machines, such as levers and pulleys. We will look at the forces involved in these machines.

There are forces at work even in things that are still. The arch of this bridge seems to lean at an unnatural angle. However, the force of gravity trying to pull the arch over is balanced by the pulling force of the cables supporting the arch.

CHAPTER 2

Speed and direction

How do we describe motion? If we say, "Nick throws a fast ball to Harriet," we can tell some things about the motion of the ball. If we know where Nick and Harriet are, we can tell what direction the ball travels in, while "fast" tells us something about its speed. When we want to describe any kind of motion, we need to know its speed and direction.

Speed

Speed is how fast something moves. To measure the speed of an object, we need to measure the distance it travels in a particular length of time. Suppose that, in the example above, Nick is standing 33 feet (10 meters) from Harriet and the ball takes a second to get to Harriet. Then the speed of the ball is 33 feet per second (10 meters per second).

Of course, things don't often travel at a constant speed. If you go on a road trip, the speed you travel at varies. However, if you know how far you have traveled, and you time how long the trip takes, you can work out an average speed for the journey. For instance, if your trip was 50 miles (80 kilometers), and it took 80 minutes, your average speed would be 0.62 miles per minute or 37 mph (1 kilometer per minute or 60 km/h). However, if the same journey took one minute, your average speed would be 50 miles per minute or 3,000 mph (80 kilometers per minute or 4,800 km/h), and you were probably traveling in a rocket!

! AMAZING FACTS

Top speed

The fastest that any vehicle has traveled is about 150,000 mph (240,000 km/h). The *Helios 2* space probe reached this speed when **orbiting** the Sun. The fastest a human has traveled is 24,816 mph (39,937 km/h). *Apollo 10* reached this speed on its practice Moon flight.

PLOTTING A CAR'S SPEED

One way to show the speed of a car on a journey is to plot a graph of distance traveled against time. A straight diagonal line indicates constant speed, a curved line shows the car speeding up or slowing down. The steeper the slope of the line, the faster the car is going. In this example, the car speeds up until it is traveling fast, then slows to a stop.

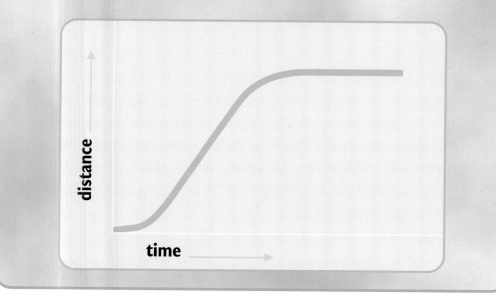

Direction

If an airplane traveled from New York at a constant 350 miles per hour (560 kilometers per hour) for 10 hours, it could reach London. However, if the airplane flew south for $2\frac{1}{2}$ hours, then east for $2\frac{1}{2}$ hours, then $2\frac{1}{2}$ hours north, and finally $2\frac{1}{2}$ hours west, it would end up back in New York. This shows that if we want to describe the motion of an object, it is not enough to know its speed—we need to know the direction, too.

When we talk about directions, we need a reference point to take directions from. In the example above, the reference point is New York. We also need a way of indicating directions that is clear. The example above uses compass directions.

Velocity

A lot of the time, "**velocity**" seems to be used as another word for speed. However, in science it has a specific meaning. The velocity of a moving object is its speed in a particular direction. As we have already seen, speed on its own is not enough to describe the motion of an object—direction is needed as well. So velocity is a better description of the motion of an object.

We can see how this works if we look at the motion of the airplane flying from New York mentioned on page 7. The average speed of the airplane over the whole trip is 350 mph (560 km/h). However, this doesn't help to tell us where the airplane is. The velocity measurements are different. The velocity is a measure of the distance and speed traveled from the original point of departure. Look at the chart and you will see that each velocity measurement gives the location of the airplane and the distance from New York. After the first leg of the journey, the average velocity is 350 mph (560 km/h) south (of New York). After the second leg, the average velocity is 492 mph (792 km/h) southeast (of New York), after the third leg it is 350 mph (560 km/h) east (of New York), and after the fourth, the velocity is zero, because the airplane is back where it started.

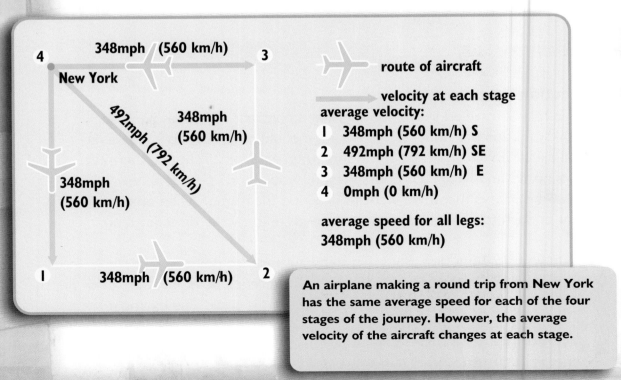

route of aircraft

velocity at each stage

average velocity:
1 348mph (560 km/h) S
2 492mph (792 km/h) SE
3 348mph (560 km/h) E
4 0mph (0 km/h)

average speed for all legs:
348mph (560 km/h)

An airplane making a round trip from **New York** has the same average speed for each of the four stages of the journey. However, the average velocity of the aircraft changes at each stage.

Acceleration is a change in velocity rather than a change of speed. Acceleration can be a change of speed, a change of direction, or a change of both speed and direction. So when a car goes around a bend in the road, it is accelerating, even if its speed stays the same.

Changing velocity

When a car pulls away from a curb, its velocity changes—it accelerates (gets faster). **Acceleration** is a change in velocity. If the velocity is measured in feet per second (ft./s) (or meters per second (m/s)), acceleration is measured in feet per second per second (ft./s/s) (meters per second per second (m/s/s)). Let's say that after 1 second, the car is traveling at 6.5 ft./s (2 m/s), after 2 seconds, it is traveling at 13 ft./s (4 m/s). In 3 seconds, it has reached 20 ft./s (6 m/s), and so on. The speed increases by 6.5 ft./s (2 m/s) each second, so the acceleration is 6.5 ft./s/s second (2 m/s/s).

If the car slows down and stops at a traffic light, its velocity is changing, so this is also acceleration. But in this case, the velocity is getting less, so this is called **negative acceleration.**

Dragsters are designed for acceleration. The cars race in pairs on a straight course, usually a quarter of a mile. The fastest cars take less than 5 seconds for the race, and reach speeds of 300 mph (482 km/h).

CHAPTER 3

Moving forces

In Chapter 2, we looked at how to describe motion through speed and direction. For any kind of motion to happen, we need forces. Whenever something starts or stops, speeds up, slows down, or changes direction, a force must be involved.

Changing speed

When a car drives away usually, it is not obvious what forces are involved in making it move. If a car will not start, the driver might try to push-start it. With push-starting, the forces are clearer. All the people helping (it usually takes at least two) get behind the car and push as hard as they can. As they push, the car slowly moves in the direction they are pushing.

Push-starting a car illustrates the general rule that when an object accelerates, the force producing the **acceleration** acts in the direction that the object is moving. The force does not have to be a push from behind—it could be a pull from in front. A horse pulls a cart from the front, and a tractor pulls a plow.

FORCE, MASS, AND ACCELERATION

The acceleration of an object depends on the force used to accelerate it and its mass. This can be written as an equation:

$$F = ma$$

This equation can be rearranged if you want to know the acceleration or the mass rather than the force:

$$a = F/m \qquad m = F/a$$

Slowing something down is also accelerating, but in a negative direction, so a force acting in the opposite direction to the movement also accelerates an object. A horse wanting to slow down a cart leans back into the shafts. This puts a force on the shafts in the opposite direction to the cart's movement.

The amount of force used to move an object will affect how fast it accelerates. A large force will make something accelerate fast, a small force will produce less acceleration. The acceleration of an object also depends on its **mass**. A car is heavy, so it needs a large force to get it moving. Much less force is needed to accelerate a bicycle.

Push-starting a car takes a lot of force. But in strength events, competitors have to pull-start a truck, or even an airplane, by themselves.

Changing direction

Whenever a force acts on a moving object, it causes the object to accelerate; that is, it changes speed or direction. So if we discover that an object is accelerating, we know there must be a force acting on it.

Imagine swinging a ball attached to a string about your head. You would have an object that is traveling at a constant speed, but is always changing direction. The ball would be constantly accelerating.

In this example, it is easy to see that the force accelerating the ball comes from you. As the ball goes around, you have to constantly pull on the string to keep it circling.

If we draw a diagram showing what is happening, we can see that whatever point the ball is at on its travels, the force pulling on it is acting at right angles to its direction of movement, correcting its path so it keeps going in a circle. It is a general rule that a force acting at right angles to a moving object will change its direction, but not its speed.

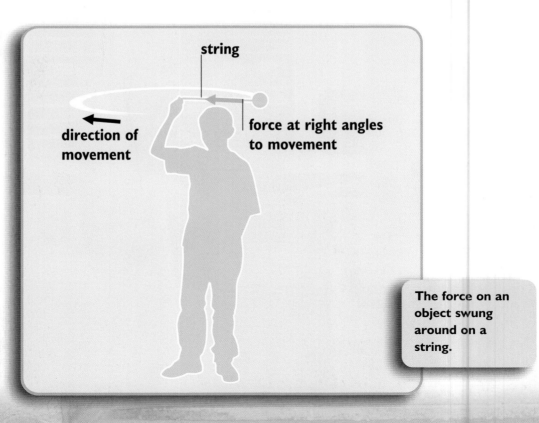

string

direction of movement

force at right angles to movement

The force on an object swung around on a string.

On this merry-go-round ride, the chains provide a pulling force that stops the chairs from flying off in a straight line.

Changing speed and direction

A force at any other angle than in line with the movement or at right angles will affect both the object's speed and its direction. You can sometimes see an example of this in a hockey match. The puck comes sliding across the ice toward the goal, but the goalkeeper has it covered. Then an attacker zooms across the rink and hits the puck at an angle. The new force makes the puck shoot off much faster and at the new angle. It slips past the keeper into the net.

! AMAZING FACTS

The Rotor

You may be familiar with **an amusement park** ride called the **Gravitron**. You walk into a circular room, like a big drum. You stand against the wall, and the room begins to spin, faster and faster. Then suddenly the floor under your feet starts to drop away. But you do not fall—you stay stuck to the wall.

When you are on the **Gravitron**, it feels as if a force is pushing you against the outside wall. However, what is happening is that your body is trying to go in a straight line, wanting to fling itself out of the circle. The force of the wall pushes against your body, toward the center of the space, to keep you going around. The balancing of these forces keeps your body almost fixed to its spot.

Things stay as they are...

If you are riding in a car and the driver has to brake quickly, you feel as if you are flung forward against your seat belt. Or if you go fast around a tight corner, you feel as if you are being pressed over to the outside of the curve. Both these effects are caused by **inertia**.

Inertia is produced by the tendency of things to stay as they are. An object moving at a uniform speed will continue to do so until a force acts on it (see page 16). In this case, the object is your body. When the driver puts on the car's brakes, a strong **friction** force on the wheels suddenly slows the car down. But the brakes act on the car, not on you. The car slows down, but you keep going forward until a force acts to slow you down. That force comes from the seat belt you are wearing. It presses against your chest and stops your forward motion. If you weren't wearing a seat belt, you could crash into the windshield.

When the car is going around a curve, inertia once again produces the effects on your body. The driver turns the car's wheels to steer it around the curve, but you keep going in a straight line, rather than turning.

Inertia and momentum

An object's inertia depends on its **mass**. The more massive something is, the more force is needed to change its **velocity**. For example, when you are push-starting a car, getting it moving is very hard work. The car has lots of mass, and so it takes a large force to get the car going. Once the car is moving, keeping it going only needs enough force to overcome friction, so pushing it becomes easier.

(i) INERTIA IN SPACE

Inertia depends on mass, not weight, so it is not affected by **gravity**. If you were **orbiting** Earth in a spacecraft, it would be just as hard to push a car as on Earth, even though the car would be weightless.

Momentum is a measure of how difficult it is to change the velocity of an object. The more momentum something has, the harder it is to change its velocity. Changing an object's velocity means changing its speed, changing its direction, or both. Momentum equals velocity times mass, so the larger an object's mass, or the faster it is moving, the bigger its momentum.

In this crash test, the dummy "driver" is protected by a seat belt and an air bag. However, the dummy in the back seat has no seat belt. When the car suddenly stops, the inertia of the rear-seat dummy throws it forward.

CHAPTER 4

Resisting movement

Two of the greatest scientists ever, Galileo Galilei and Sir Isaac Newton, both thought that if an object is traveling with a constant **velocity**, it needs no force to keep it going—it will travel at that constant velocity until another force acts on it. Yet, if you put a book down on the carpet and give it a push, it will travel a short distance and then stop. Were these two scientists wrong? Or is something else going on?

It seems common sense that a book will not move across a carpet forever if you give it a single push. The book and the carpet rub against each other, and this slows the book down very quickly. But Galileo and Newton were not wrong. They said that an object will move with constant velocity until another force acts on it. As soon as you start pushing on the book, another force starts acting to oppose the motion. The rubbing of the carpet against the book creates a force known as **friction**, which acts in the opposite direction to the book's movement and soon brings it to a stop.

A portrait of Galileo Galilei, painted around 1610.

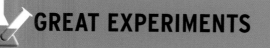

GREAT EXPERIMENTS

Galileo on motion

Between 1604 and 1607, the Italian scientist, Galileo Galilei (1564-1642), conducted several experiments on motion using a pair of ramps facing each other and a bronze ball. When Galileo rolled the ball down one ramp, he found that it rose to almost the same height up the ramp placed opposite it. However, he found that as the slope of the second ramp became gentler and longer, the ball did not come quite so close to the height it was released from. Galileo reasoned that the reason for this was friction: on a gentler slope, the ball had to travel farther, and so friction had more chance to act. He suggested that if friction could be eliminated, the ball would reach the same height that it was released from, even on a very gentle slope.

Galileo found that if he made the second ramp slope more gently, the ball still rose to about the same height, but it had to travel farther to get there. Taking this one step further, Galileo asked himself, "What happens if the second ramp keeps getting shallower?" The ball would have to roll farther and farther to reach the same height. Eventually, if the second ramp was flat, the ball would keep rolling endlessly. This does not happen in real life, because the forces of friction stop the ball. However, his experiments led Galileo to the conclusion that an object with constant velocity will keep on going unless it is acted on by another force.

A rollercoaster is like an extended version of Galileo's ramp experiment. The cars are pulled up the first hill, but after that, they are not powered at all. Each hill on the track is almost as high as the one before it.

What is friction?

Wherever two surfaces move against each other, there is **friction**. The force of friction acts in the opposite direction to the movement: if the movement is forward, friction acts backward.

Roughness also affects the amount of friction between two surfaces. It needs less force to slide a book across a glass tabletop than to slide a brick across a piece of rough concrete. Some materials, such as rubber, are naturally "sticky" and have high friction.

Friction-type forces also slow down objects moving through liquids or gases. Boats and submarines moving through the water are slowed by water resistance, while aircraft are slowed by air resistance. Air resistance and water resistance are sometimes called "drag."

Friction and speed

Friction is a force that increases with speed. The friction between two solid materials is proportional to speed: at a speed of 32 ft./s (10 m/s), the friction is twice as much as at a speed of 16 ft./s (5 m/s). However, the drag caused by air resistance is not proportional to speed. It is much greater at high speeds than at low speeds.

There is also a difference between the force needed to start off an object that is stationary (**static** friction) and the force needed to overcome friction once it is moving (**kinetic** friction). The force needed to overcome static friction is greater than the force needed to counteract kinetic friction.

There is a small amount of give in the **couplings** between the trucks in a freight train. When the train starts up, the trucks start moving one by one, rather than all together. This means that the locomotive only has to overcome the static friction of one truck at a time, rather than that of the whole train.

Spacecraft re-entry

When a spacecraft comes back into Earth's atmosphere from space, it is traveling at high speed. Friction between the spacecraft and the atmosphere helps slow the spacecraft down, but it also generates huge amounts of heat. Most spacecraft have a heat shield that slowly burns up and flakes away as it heats up. The pieces that flake off carry away some of the heat. The Space Shuttle heat shield, however, is made of tiles with incredible insulation properties, which soak up much of the heat.

During re-entry, the Space Shuttle soaks up so much heat that it is connected to a fridge-style cooling system after landing to cool it down.

Problems of friction

Often friction is something we want to avoid, because it wastes energy. Any object moving on land has to overcome both surface friction and air resistance. If you are pedaling a bicycle at a steady speed on a flat road, all the work you do is to overcome friction and drag. Aircraft have to overcome air resistance, and boats have to overcome water resistance.

In car engines and all kinds of other machines, friction does not just waste energy. Friction between the surfaces of machine parts causes them to heat up, and also wears them down.

Reducing friction

Although **friction** can be a big problem in vehicles and machinery, there are many ways to reduce it. Wheels are one solution to cutting down surface friction. Wheels roll over the surface and produces less friction than sliding.

In machinery, lubrication reduces friction. A thin layer of oil or grease between two metal surfaces drastically reduces the friction between them. Where two surfaces move a lot against each other (for instance, an axle and a wheel), bearings reduce friction even more. Bearings (small balls or cylinders) are placed between the moving surfaces. The bearings roll instead of sliding, and this produces less friction.

Streamlining

For vehicles that need to reduce air or water resistance, the answer is streamlining. When water or air moves smoothly over an object, it greatly reduces drag, so vehicles are designed with a shape that moves smoothly through the air or water. A streamlined shape is usually narrow at the front and has smooth lines, but the best shape varies, depending on the speed of the vehicle moves.

! AMAZING FACTS

Bumpy surface for a smoother ride

Until recently, conventional wisdom has been that smooth surfaces improve the flow of air or water over the surface of an object. However, studies on sharks and dolphins have found that these animals either have bumps on their skin (sharks) or create them as they swim (dolphins), and yet their water resistance is better than that of a smooth, streamlined object. As a result of this research, scientists have been testing surfaces with carefully designed surface bumps to try and reduce drag in air or water. In fact, a team of Swedish scientists has found that a surface covered in pill-sized bumps produces up to ten times less drag than a smooth surface.

Wind tunnels are used to test cars and aircraft to see how smoothly air flows around them. Air is blown through the tunnel at high speed, and special photography shows the air flow.

When friction is useful

Although friction is sometimes a problem, we could not manage without it. Anyone who has tried to walk on ice in smooth-soled shoes will know that friction between your shoes and the ground is really helpful. Animals, cars, trucks, trains, and anything else moving on land all rely on friction to move around. Friction is also essential for stopping. Brakes deliberately create friction to slow vehicles down.

Many other things rely on friction. If there was no friction, everything would fall apart. Nails would fall out of wood, screws and bolts would come unfastened, and velcro would be completely useless. Socks would always be falling down! All kinds of sports would be impossible without friction. In soccer, the goalkeeper would not be able to hold the ball, and in baseball, every catch would slip through the players' fingers. It would not be possible to sand wood, tie shoelaces, or strike a match.

What causes drag?

Air and water resistance are caused by the behavior of the particles (**atoms** and **molecules**) that make up air and water. The particles in water are quite closely packed together, but they are not still—they are continually moving around and colliding with each other. Air particles are much more spread out, but they move faster—around 1,100 miles per hour (1,800 kilometers per hour). As a solid object moves through air or water, it has to push through these moving particles, and this causes drag.

Air pressure

In a shoe box with the lid on, the air particles inside the box are zooming around at high speed. Every time one of the particles hits the wall of the box, it exerts a force. The force is tiny, but there are billions of collisions every second. Together, these add up to a substantial force pushing on the box walls. If we measure the force over a fixed area of the box, we will have a measure of the pressure of air inside. Pressure is measured in units of force, or **newtons** (N), per unit area (square meter). This unit is usually called the **pascal** (Pa).

🧪 GREAT EXPERIMENTS

Von Guericke's brass ball

In 1650, the German scientist, Otto von Guericke, invented the vacuum pump, which made it possible to pump all the air out of a container. Von Guericke experimented with two brass hemispheres (half-balls) that fitted snugly together. Once the air was pumped out from between them, the two halves were held together strongly by the outside air pressure. In one famous experiment in 1663, von Guericke harnessed teams of eight horses to either side of the brass ball, but they could not pull hard enough to separate the two halves.

Von Guericke (1602-1686) shown with his famous "Magdeburg Spheres."

Earth is covered in a layer of air about 4 miles (6 kilometers) thick. Air is light, but it still has **mass**, and **gravity** pulls it down as it does all other objects. The weight of the air above presses on the air at ground level, and compresses it. The air presses on the ground and on all objects on Earth's surface. The pressure is about 100,000 pascals (Pa), or a force of 100,000 N (about the weight of a bus) on every square meter. We do not normally feel air pressure, because the air presses equally on us from all sides, so there is no overall force.

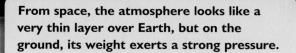

From space, the atmosphere looks like a very thin layer over Earth, but on the ground, its weight exerts a strong pressure.

CHAPTER 5

The force of gravity

Some forces do not need to come into contact with an object to affect it—they act at a distance. When it comes to acting at a distance, no force compares to **gravity**. The Sun is 93 million miles (150 million kilometers) away, yet its gravity pulls strongly on Earth.

Mutual attraction

On Earth, gravity pulls everything toward the ground. More generally, gravity is a force that attracts everything toward everything else. The gravitational "pull" of an object depends on its **mass**. The more massive something is, the more strongly its gravity acts. We feel Earth's gravity because it is very massive, but nothing else nearby, such as the Moon or the planets, has enough mass for us to feel its pull.

The gravitational attraction between Earth and the Moon keeps the Moon in orbit around Earth.

Gravity and distance

Every object has a point known as its **center of mass**. For **spherical** objects like Earth, the center of mass is also the center of gravity. Earth's center of gravity is the center of Earth, about 3,963 miles (6,378 kilometers) away from the surface.

The force of gravity quickly becomes weaker the farther away you get from an object. A satellite in **orbit** 3,963 miles (6,378 kilometers) above Earth would be twice as far from the center of gravity as we are on the surface. However, gravity at this point is only a quarter as strong as on Earth's surface.

Weight and mass

Weight and mass are two different things. While we will say that a piece of cheese will weigh just over one pound (0.5 kilogram), in scientific terms, you cannot have a weight of half a kilo. A kilogram is a measure of mass, which is the amount of matter (stuff) in an object. Instead, the weight of an object is the force of gravity acting on it. Weight is measured in **newtons**. The force of gravity is close to constant all over Earth, so the weight of something in newtons is roughly its mass in kilograms multiplied by 10. However, as soon as you leave Earth, this calculation changes. If we put the same piece of cheese into orbit around Earth, the cheese will be weightless—there is no overall force of gravity acting on it. However, its mass does not change—it still "weighs" half a kilogram.

ⓘ MASS AND WEIGHT

The mass of the lump of cheese is always 0.5 kg, but its weight, measured in newtons (N), changes depending on where it is.

	Earth	Earth orbit	Moon	Jupiter
Mass	0.5 kg	0.5 kg	0.5 kg	0.5 kg
Weight (weight [force] = mass x acceleration due to gravity)	5 N	0.0 N	0.8 N	12.5 N

The free fall force

Gravity is a force that acts toward the center of Earth, and it is the same all over the world. But what exactly is it? How do we measure the force of gravity? One way to start is to think about what happens if you fall from a great height.

If you jump out of a plane without opening a parachute, the only force acting on you is gravity. (There is also air resistance, but at first it is very small). We showed earlier that a force acting on an object makes it **accelerate**. Gravity acts downward, so you begin to accelerate toward the ground.

A skydiver jumping from a plane will continue to fall quicker with every second that passes, until he or she opens her parachute.

As you continue to fall, gravity continues to act with the same force, so you continue to accelerate, going faster and faster at a constant rate. Because gravity is the same all over the world, the acceleration produced by gravity on an object in free fall is always the same—32.1 ft./s/s (9.8 m/s/s), or 33 ft./s/s (10 m/s/s) to the nearest whole number. So after 1 second, an object in free fall will travel at 33 ft./s (10 m/s), after 2 seconds it will travel at 65 ft./s/s (20 m/s/s), and so on. The acceleration due to gravity is called "g" or g-force.

Scientists use the g-force for measuring the acceleration that pilots experience when aircraft dive and turn, or astronauts feel when rockets take off. Most people can cope with forces of 5 g (five times gravity). With the help of specially designed g-suits, pilots and astronauts can work for a time under forces of 9 g. On a rollercoaster ride at a fairground, passengers experience accelerations of 3 g or more.

! AMAZING FACTS

Zero gravity on Earth

Astronauts learning how to cope in space are trained in aircraft flights that simulate zero gravity. The aircraft first climbs steeply, then cuts the power and starts to dive. It is like being on a rollercoaster. As a rollercoaster goes over the top of a hump, there is a moment when you feel weightless. Similarly, as the aircraft goes "over the top" in its curved flight, there is a short period of zero gravity.

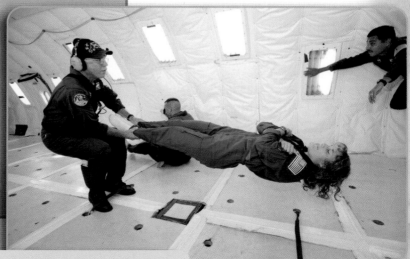

A reduced gravity session for trainee astronauts.

Gravity beyond Earth

The movements of stars, planets, and moons are all controlled by **gravity**. The planets and moons of our own Solar System are held together by the gravity of the Sun. The planets are in **orbit** around the Sun, while the moons orbit the planets. So how exactly does gravity act to keep the planets in orbit?

Falling orbit

In his book on gravity, Sir Isaac Newton explains how orbits work through a thought experiment. He asks readers to imagine firing a cannon from a very high place. If you fire it using a single charge of gunpowder, the cannonball goes a long way, but eventually falls to the ground. With two charges of gunpowder, the cannonball goes much farther. With three charges, the cannonball goes even farther, falling toward Earth in a long curve. However, Earth's surface is curved, too, and as the cannonball falls, Earth falls away beneath it. The cannonball keeps falling and falling, but it never hits Earth, because Earth curves away from under it. The cannonball goes into orbit.

GREAT SCIENTISTS

Sir Isaac Newton

The law of gravity was discovered by the English scientist, Sir Isaac Newton. In his book *Principia*, published in 1687, Newton showed that every object in the universe is attracted to every other object. Newton's law showed that the force of gravity on Earth is the same force that acts on the planets, the Sun, stars, and galaxies far beyond Earth.

A portrait of Sir Isaac Newton.

Like the cannonball, every satellite (a satellite is anything in orbit around something else) is in permanent free fall. The satellite has enough forward speed to just balance the force of gravity trying to pull it toward the ground. Out in space, there is no air resistance to slow the satellite down, so it keeps orbiting for a very long time.

However, space is not completely empty, and tiny pieces of dust and other material gradually slow the satellite down. Eventually, the satellite either falls to Earth, or it uses a small booster rocket to get back up to speed.

Universal glue

Gravity holds Earth and other planets in orbit around the Sun, but it doesn't stop there. The Sun is one of billions of stars in our galaxy, the Milky Way. Gravity keeps this huge cluster of stars together. On an even larger scale, astronomers have found whole clusters of galaxies held together in a loose group by gravitational attraction. Gravity is a "universal glue."

Our galaxy, the Milky Way, is a vast disk of stars circling around a central core or hub. Scientists think that the center of the Milky Way contains a supermassive **black hole**. This black hole has the **mass** of more than 3 million Suns concentrated down into a single point.

CHAPTER 6

Balanced and unbalanced forces

It is rare for there to be only one force on an object. More often there are two or more forces acting at once. If an object is still or in steady motion, it is usually because there is a balance of forces acting on it, rather than no force at all. When two (or more) forces are not in balance, there is an overall force that produces a change of movement.

Balanced and still

A simple example of balanced forces is a person standing still. We have already come across one force acting on that person—that person's weight. **Gravity** pulls a 90-lb. (40-kg) person toward the center of Earth with a force of about 400 **newtons**. However, since the person is not moving there must be another force opposing the pull of gravity. This force is produced by the ground. The ground does not actively push the person upward. It simply stops the person from falling, because it is solid.

Forces in water

Forces can be balanced in the water as well as on land. When a boat is floating on still water, the force of the boat's weight pressing down on the water is balanced by another force, known as **upthrust**. This is the force of the water pressing upward against the boat's weight. You can feel the force of the upthrust if you try to press an air-filled plastic ball under the water. It is hard to push the ball completely under the water, and if you let go, it pops straight back up again.

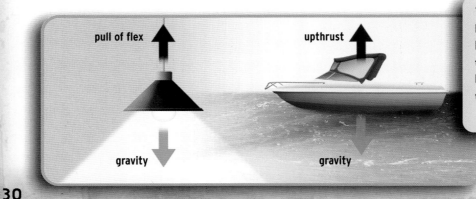

pull of flex

upthrust

gravity

gravity

Two examples of balanced forces: a lamp hanging from the ceiling and a boat floating on the water.

Things float better in salty water than they do in fresh water. This is because salty water is more **dense**, so the upthrust produced by salty water is greater.

Forces on structures

Forces on a still object seem simple and obvious at first glance. However, engineers spend a great deal of time working out the forces on static objects. Suppose you are the engineer responsible for building a large dam. What will the forces on the dam be, and what design and materials should you use to make sure that the dam is safe? Engineers building everything from playground equipment to suspension bridges have to take into account all the forces on a structure, and make sure that they are balanced.

ARCHES

Heavy materials, such as stone and concrete, are very strong when compressed, but much weaker under tension (being stretched or bent). Arches built of stone or concrete are much stronger than flat beams. When there is a weight on a beam, the bottom part of it is stretched (under tension), and it is not as strong. However, a weight on top of an arch compresses the material that makes up the arch instead of stretching it, so it becomes stronger when it carries a weight.

An arch structure is not strong until the stone at the top of the arch, known as the **keystone**, is in place. As it is being built, the arch has to be supported, either with cables from above or with scaffolding (known as centering) from below.

Balanced but moving

If something is moving at constant speed, the forces on it are balanced. A good example of balanced forces on the move is a bicycle moving at constant speed. The force of the ground pushing upward balances the weight of the bicycle due to **gravity**, and the force with which the cyclist pedals the bike forward is just enough to balance the drag on the bike due to **friction** and air resistance.

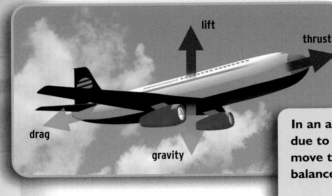

In an aircraft flying at a steady speed, the downward for due to gravity is balanced by the lift produced as the wir move through the air. The forward thrust of the engines balanced by the backward force of air resistance (drag).

Changing shape

One other thing that forces can do is change the shape of something. If, for instance, you hang an object on a spring, the force of the object's weight will pull on the spring and stretch it. At some point, the elastic force trying to shorten the spring will be equal to the force of gravity pulling on the object. When this happens, the forces are balanced and the spring will stop stretching. If you take the weight off the spring, the forces will become unbalanced again and it will bounce back.

NEWTON'S LAWS

As well as explaining gravity, Sir Isaac Newton also worked out three laws that together explain all kinds of motion. We have already come across these laws in the book. The First Law of Motion states that an object at rest or moving at a constant **velocity** will continue in that state until acted on by another force (see page 16). The Second Law is the relationship between force, mass and **acceleration**: $F = ma$ (see page 10). The Third Law, as we have just seen, is that all actions have an equal and opposite reaction.

Paired forces

In all cases where forces are balanced, they act in pairs—for instance, gravity and lift, thrust and drag. These pairs are known as **action-reaction pairs**. Any action has an equal and opposite reaction.

If you are playing tennis, for instance, and hit the ball hard, as soon as your racket pushes the ball one way, the ball pushes back the other way. It may seem as if the forces cannot be equal, because the ball goes flying, but you do not go anywhere. However, the **mass** of you plus your tennis racket is much greater than the mass of the tennis ball, so a force that sends the tennis ball flying has little effect on you. The situation is reversed if, for instance, you push on a wall. The wall is very massive and shows no effect from your action (the push), whereas you are pushed backward by the wall's reaction.

A rocket relies on action and reaction for its power. The rocket pushes hot gases out backward at high speed. The force of the gases traveling backward produces a forward reaction force on the rocket.

Unbalanced forces

When the forces on an object are not in balance, you get a change in movement: the object may change speed, change direction, or both. The actual effect produced depends on the forces acting on the object. If we look first at two unbalanced forces acting in the same or opposite directions, you can add the forces together, or subtract one from another, to work out the overall force on the object.

If two forces act in the same direction, they add together. In relay speed-skating, when pairs of skaters switch, the skater who is finishing pushes his partner to pass on his **momentum**. The starting skater gets extra acceleration from this pushing force.

For instance, suppose that you stand on a skateboard at the top of a slope. **Friction** between the ground and the skateboard wheels will tend to stop you from moving. Acting in the opposite direction is the force of **gravity**, tending to pull you down the slope. The overall force on the skateboard is the force of gravity minus the force due to friction. Unless the surface is rough or the slope is shallow, the force of gravity will be stronger than the friction force, and the skateboard will begin to **accelerate** down the slope.

Skydiving

A skydiver is a parachutist who jumps out of a plane and falls freely for a time before opening his or her parachute. What happens during a jump is an interesting mix of balanced and unbalanced forces.

As skydivers leave the plane, they are in free fall—gravity pulls them downward with an acceleration of 33 ft./s/s (10 m/s/s). However, as they gather speed, air resistance begins to oppose the force of gravity. As the skydivers' speed increases, air resistance grows and grows. Eventually, it pushes upward with the same force as gravity pulls downward—the forces are balanced. The skydivers no longer accelerate, but they continue to fall very fast. When a falling object stops accelerating, it has reached "terminal **velocity**."

> The changes in the forces acting on a skydiver during a jump. In (b) and (d) the forces are the same. However, at (b) the skydiver is traveling at about 110 mph (180 km/h), while at (d) he is falling much more slowly.

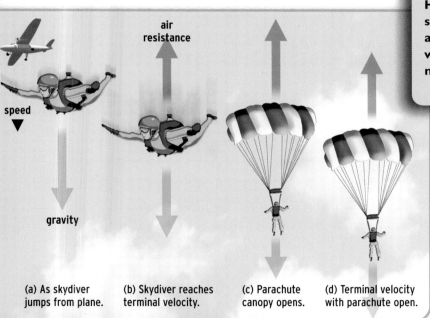

air resistance

speed ▼

gravity

(a) As skydiver jumps from plane.

(b) Skydiver reaches terminal velocity.

(c) Parachute canopy opens.

(d) Terminal velocity with parachute open.

When the skydivers open their parachutes, the forces suddenly change. The large area of a parachute has a much greater air resistance than a skydiver's body. Now the upward force of air resistance is much greater than the downward force of gravity, and the parachutists begins to slow down. As they slow, air resistance decreases again. Eventually, air resistance matches the pull of gravity once again. The parachutists now reach terminal velocity again, but at a slower rate.

Changing direction

If one force acts in a direction that is not in line with another force, it will affect the direction the object is moving in. When there are several forces acting on an object in different directions, it can be difficult to work out what effect they have. However, no matter how many forces are involved, the forces combine together or cancel out to produce a single force on the object in a particular direction.

One example of this is a thrown ball. When a ball has been thrown, there are basically two forces acting on it—air resistance and **gravity**. Gravity acts vertically downward, with the same force, throughout the ball's flight. The force of air resistance on the ball changes as the ball's speed and direction change, but it always acts to slow the ball down. The result is that the ball travels in a curved path to the ground. Working out the exact shape of this curve is a difficult mathematical problem. However, we can say that all through the ball's flight, the overall force on it must be acting downward and against the direction of motion. This is clear because the ball is continually slowing down and curving downward.

Colliding forces

When two objects collide, the force of the collision depends on the **momentum** of the objects. Two massive objects moving slowly will collide with a similar force to two less massive objects moving faster. In any collision, the overall momentum before and afterward is the same. Momentum is simply transferred from one object to another.

(i) MOMENTUM SPORTS

Many sports rely on skillfully transferring momentum from one object to another. In all ball games, players try to accurately change the momentum of the ball with a bat, racket, or stick, or with their hands or feet. If the ball is large and fairly heavy, as in soccer, more force is needed to change its momentum.

A good example of collision forces is the bumper cars at a fair. When driving along in a bumper car, another car will often come charging up from behind and bash into the back of you. Your car gives a jolt and shoots forward, and the car that hit you comes to a stop. There has been a transfer of momentum from one car to the other.

When tennis players serve, they swing their racket at high speed toward the ball. The racket transfers much of its momentum to the ball, which can leave the racket at a speed of 140 miles per hour (225 kilometers per hour).

CHAPTER 7

Moving machines

Humans are not particularly strong or fast-moving, but we have found ways of using machines to increase the force we can use, and to make things move faster. In this chapter, we will look at how levers and other simple machines help us do everything from cutting our nails to building dams.

Ramps

Perhaps the simplest machine of all is a ramp. Many stores today have ramps to make it easier for wheelchairs or buggies to get into the store. It is much easier to push a wheelchair or buggy up a ramp than to lift it vertically. To lift a wheelchair vertically, you might need a force of 800 **newtons**, but you would need only 200 newtons to push it up a ramp. However, lifting the wheelchair vertically would travel less distance, so the amount of work in both cases would be the same.

Levers

Levers are very useful and versatile machines. A **lever** is a long rod or beam that can swing about a **pivot** point. One simple kind of lever is a seesaw. For a seesaw to work well, the people on either end must be about the same weight. Otherwise, the heavier person will press their end down, and the lighter person will be stuck up in the air.

Our arm and leg joints are levers, but they are set up to give large amounts of movement, rather than moving a large load with a small effort. A javelin thrower makes maximum use of this movement when he or she throws the javelin.

It is possible for a light person and a heavy person to balance a seesaw, if the heavier person sits closer to the pivot than the lighter person. This illustrates the basic principle behind all levers. In any lever, there is one force, called the **effort,** acting at one point on the lever and another opposing force, called the **load,** at another point. When the lever is in balance, effort times distance from the pivot equals load times distance from the pivot.

So if a heavy load is close to a pivot, and the effort is far from the pivot, the load can be moved with a small force.

(i) JUST A MOMENT...

When a lever is in balance, the turning force produced on one side of the lever must balance the turning force on the other side. If the turning forces are not balanced, the lever moves. The turning force is known as the **moment** (M). The moment on each side of the pivot is the force on the lever multiplied by the distance of that force from the pivot:

moment (M) = force (F) x distance from pivot (d)

The unit of measurement for moments is newton meters (Nm).

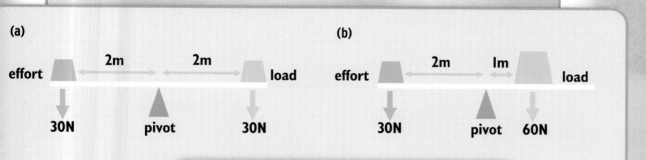

(a)

effort   2m   2m   load

30N   pivot   30N

(b)

effort   2m   1m   load

30N   pivot 60N

How a lever works. In **(a)**, the load and effort are the same, and are an equal distance from the pivot. The lever balances. In **(b)** the load is twice as big as the effort, but half the distance from the pivot. Again the lever balances. In both **(a)** and **(b)**, the moments on both sides of the pivot are the same—that is, 60 Nm.

Useful levers

Levers are used in many ways. Most often they are used to gain a mechanical advantage—this means using a small effort to lift a large load. A crowbar is a simple example. Crowbars are used to lift heavy weights or to lever the tops off crates. The end of the crowbar that goes under the load is very short, so it is close to the **pivot**. The other arm of the lever is long, so a small effort on this end produces a large lifting force.

Many types of lever work in pairs, with a pivot connecting them. A pair of scissors is a pair of levers, as are pliers, tweezers, and nutcrackers. Other levers have both the load and the effort on the same side of the pivot. In a wheelbarrow, for example, the wheel is the pivot, and the heavy load is placed almost over it. The handles are farther from the pivot, so the effort needed to lift the load is much less.

A heavy load of wood is moved easily using a wheelbarrow, because the load is above the pivot (the wheel) and the long handles give more leverage.

MECHANICAL ADVANTAGE

The mechanical advantage of a lever or another simple machine is the amount that the machine multiplies the force put into it. For a lever, the mechanical advantage is the distance from the pivot to the effort divided by the distance from the pivot to the load. So if the load is 20 in. (50 cm) from the pivot while the effort is 80 in. (200 cm) away, the mechanical advantage is 80/20 = 4 (200/50 = 4).

Screws

The thread of a screw is basically a thin strip, like a ramp, wrapped around in a spiral. On a nut or a screw, the thread has many turns, so the "ramp" is very long. As a result, screws and bolts grip with tremendous strength.

Screw threads are used in many devices besides screws and bolts. The spiral thread on a drill helps to bore holes, but it also provides a channel for removing waste material, such as sawdust. Taps have a screw thread to close off a water pipe securely, and some car jacks use a screw thread to raise the weight of a car.

The arm of an excavator is made up of three different levers—the boom, which moves up and down; the dipper, which moves in and out; and the bucket itself, which also moves in and out. The whole cab can also rotate.

Wheels and axles

Wheels cut down the **friction** between an object and the surface it is moving over because wheels roll rather than slide. However, wheels are also force magnifiers. A turning force on the outside of a wheel produces a much larger turning force at its center. This force can be transferred to other parts of a machine using an axle.

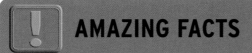

AMAZING FACTS

Roman wheel-power

For thousands of years before we began to use water turbines to generate electricity, people used large waterwheels to generate power. The power was usually used to grind wheat into flour. One of the biggest of these waterwheel "power stations" was a mill built in Roman times at Barbegal, near Arles in France. An aqueduct was used to power a complex of 16 waterwheels in two lines of eight down a hillside. The mill produced enough flour to feed at least 12,500 people—probably the population of Arles at the time.

One example of a wheel and axle is a steering wheel. The driver steers the car using the outside rim of the wheel. The force he uses to turn the steering wheel is greatly magnified in the steering shaft, which transmits the turning force to the wheels. A wrench is another simple example. When a wrench is used to turn a nut, a small turning force at one end of the wrench produces a large turning force in the nut at the other end.

Gears and belts are very versatile wheels that can be used in many different ways. A large gear connected to a small gear changes a slow rotation in one direction to a fast rotation in the other. Groups of connected gears and belts are used in bicycles, car gearboxes, lawnmowers, and all kinds of other machines.

Pulleys

Cranes, hoists, and most other lifting devices rely on pulleys. A **pulley** is basically one or more wheels and a rope. One end of the rope is fastened to the load, the other end passes through a hanging pulley and down to the ground. Pulling on the rope lifts the load.

With a single pulley, there is no mechanical advantage—the pulley does not magnify the force. However, with a second pulley the effort needed to lift the load is halved. Adding more pulley wheels increases the mechanical advantage further. However, the more pulley wheels are used, the more rope has to be pulled through to achieve the same rise in height.

Windmills rely on the wheel and axle principle to generate power. The large blades of the windmill produce a very strong rotation force at the center. This force is used to drive an electric **generator.**

CHAPTER 8

The future of forces

Now that we have looked at forces, we know that they change movement. We know that some forces need contact, but others, such as **gravity**, act at a distance. We have learned that **friction** slows us down, but it also keeps us standing and holds our socks up.

Unless we can go to deep space, we cannot escape from forces. Even when we are still, gravity pulls down on us and a reaction force from the ground pushes up. We stay still because the forces on us balance out.

Harnessing forces

We have seen how people have learned to use simple machines to gain a mechanical advantage, and to increase the force with which they can push or pull things. Today, we can use the power of the wind, water, combustion (burning), and electricity to produce very large forces indeed. We can also harness the power of the **atom**.

! AMAZING FACTS

Nuclear forces

The forces holding the **nuclei** of atoms together are enormous. If we could safely make use of these forces, we could have unlimited energy. Today's nuclear power stations produce large amounts of power, but they use **radioactive** fuels and produce wastes that remain dangerous for hundreds of years. Scientists are working on harnessing **nuclear fusion**, the nuclear reaction that happens in the Sun. In the Sun, fusion releases simply staggering amounts of energy. However, it could be 50 years or more before scientists develop a useful form of fusion on Earth.

Future forces?

In the future, what new ways will we find to use force? Two revolutions on the horizon could give us new ways to make forces work for us. Research into making robots has reached the stage where they may soon become common in the home. Robot lawnmowers are already available: soon, perhaps, we will be able to hand all kinds of household jobs over to robots.

Engineers can already build miniature robots the size of insects, like the ant shown here. In the near future, these robots may shrink much further.

The other possible revolution is the development of micromachines. It could soon be possible to build machines the size of a pollen grain. A machine this size would be able to float on a breeze, **accelerate** rapidly (because of its small **momentum**), and get into tiny spaces. If it was one of millions of tiny "microbots" with an intelligence to match a powerful modern computer, the possibilities would be huge. We saw on pages 22-23 how billions of tiny air **molecules** together produce a force of thousands of **newtons**. In the future, microbots may be able to do something similar. A large number of tiny, almost invisible microbots could produce a strong force that people can program in any way they want.

Glossary

acceleration change of the speed of an object, or its direction, or both its speed and direction.

atoms very tiny particles that make up all substances.

black hole in a black hole, a large amount of material is concentrated into a very small space. The gravity of a black hole is so strong that not even light can escape from it.

couplings connections between the trucks of a train.

dense a dense object is heavy for its size.

electromagnetism the force that makes magnets attract each other, and attracts objects of opposite electric charge toward each other.

friction a force between two objects rubbing against each other that resists the movement. Friction between two materials also generates heat.

generator a machine that creates electricity by turning a coil of wire in a magnetic field.

gravity the force that attracts all objects toward each other.

kinetic relating to movement.

mass the amount of "stuff" in an object.

molecules combinations of two or more atoms joined together by chemical bonds.

momentum a measure of how difficult it is to change the velocity of an object.

newton the unit of measurement for force.

nuclear fusion a reaction involving the nucleus of an atom, in which hydrogen atoms fuse (join together) to form helium atoms.

nucleus the central part of an atom.

orbit the path of an object like a planet around another one.

pascal the unit of measurement of pressure.

pivot the point that a lever rotates around.

radioactive a radioactive material is one in which the atoms produce radiation from the atomic nucleus.

spherical shaped like a ball.

turbine an arrangement of two or more blades around a central shaft. Turbines are usually fanlike, with many blades, or like propellers, with two or three blades.

velocity the speed of an object and the direction it is traveling in.

Further information

Books

Eyewitness Science: Force and Motion, Peter Lafferty. Dorling Kindersley and Science Museum London, 1992.

Forces, Energy and Motion, Alastair Smith. Usbourne Publishing, 2001.

Hands On Science: Forces and Motion, John Graham. Kingfisher, 2001.

Horrible Science: Fatal Forces, Nick Arnold and Tony De Saulles. Scholastic Hippo, 1997.

Science Files: Forces and Motion, Chris Oxlade. Wayland, 2005.

Science Investigations: Forces and Motion, Chris Oxlade. Wayland, 2005.

Science Topics: Forces and Motion, Peter D. Riley. Heinemann Library, 2000.

Young Oxford Library of Science: Energy and Forces, Neil Ardley. Oxford University Press, 2002.

Web sites

Due to the changing nature of Internet links, The Rosen Publishing Group, Inc., has developed an online list of Web sites related to the subject of this book. This site is updated regularly. Please use this link to access the list: www.rosenlinks.com/ps/forces/

Index